RAISED BED GARDENER'S GUIDE:

A Practical Handbook for Beginners to get a Thriving Garden With High Yield Growth and Healthy Sustainable Activity at Your Home

TAMMY SOLOMON & CLOE WYLIE

© Copyright 2020 - All rights reserved.

The content contained within this book may not be reproduced, duplicated or transmitted without direct written permission from the author or the publisher.

Under no circumstances will any blame or legal responsibility be held against the publisher, or author, for any damages, reparation, or monetary loss due to the information contained within this book. Either directly or indirectly.

Legal Notice: This book is copyright protected. This book is only for personal use. You cannot amend, distribute, sell, use, quote or paraphrase any part, or the content within this book, without the consent of the author or publisher.

Disclaimer Notice: Please note the information contained within this document is for educational and entertainment purposes only. All effort has been executed to present accurate, up to date, and reliable, complete information. No warranties of any kind are declared or implied. Readers acknowledge that the author is not engaging in the rendering of legal, financial, medical or professional advice. The content within this book has been derived from various sources. Please consult a licensed professional before attempting any techniques outlined in this book.

By reading this document, the reader agrees that under no circumstances is the author responsible for any losses, direct or indirect, which are incurred as a result of the use of information contained within this document, including, but not limited to, — errors, omissions, or inaccuracies.

Table Of Contents

Introduction 6

Chapter 1: What You Have To Know Before You Start A Raised Bed Garden 8

Chapter 2: Common Mistakes In Raised Beds Gardening 18

Chapter 3: Sustainable And Inexpensive Materials That Won't' Rot 22

Chapter 4: How To Build Your Own Raised Bed Garden 28

Chapter 5: Best Vegetables To Plant In A Raised Bed 38

Chapter 6: Defend Your Garden By Animals 46

Chapter 7: Advantages Of Gardening In Raised Beds 56

Chapter 8: Deciding On Your Raised Bed Garden 62

Chapter 9: Tips For Successful Raised Bed Gardening 66

Conclusion 80

Introduction

Raised beds allow you to plant more densely than you usually can and grow more plants in a smaller area, typically being far more productive than non-raised bed gardening, more so if you use the right soil mix.

Raised beds can be made out of pretty much anything you want, most of mine are made out of wood, but I am building one out of an old bath and have several made out of reclaimed bricks! You can use bricks, pallets, concrete, wood, metal, or anything you can get hold of, though just be careful that whatever you use doesn't contain harmful chemicals that can leach into the soil and into the vegetables you eat. This book is designed to be your complete guide to raised beds, whether you are a beginner or have been gardening for a while.

As well as learning about building and planting raised beds, you will learn how to keep pests and weeds down too, which are the bane of any gardener. You will be pleased to know that raised beds are straightforward to weed if you follow the guidelines in this book, and you can certainly reduce the risk of pests very quickly. There is a lot less maintenance with raised beds and a lot less work once they are set up.

You will also find out how you can support your plants, rotate your crops (and why it is SO important) plus succession planting, which gives you even more products from your beds.

Raised beds are a good way to garden and, once they are built, low maintenance. They are easy to work with, easy to manage, and can become an eye-catching feature of your garden. I regularly get people asking me about my raised beds, and, in my opinion, it makes a vegetable garden or allotment look beautiful and well kept. You can turn your entire vegetable plot over to raised beds or just a section of the growing area; it is up to you.

CHAPTER 1:

What you have to know before You start a raised bed garden

Select the Best Site

Most plants, especially herbs, vegetables, and some flowers, need a minimum of eight hours of sunlight every day. Once you have decided which plants you want to start with, select the site that will give your plants optimum exposure to the sun throughout the season. The area should be level and proximity to the water source will make a big difference to your chores. Remember that you will need room to move around your beds while tending them.

Decide on the Shape and Size of the Garden

When considering the size of your raised bed garden, bear in mind that all areas of it must be easily accessible to you without you having to step into any of the beds. The soil in raised beds has the advantage of staying loose and not compacted like conventional ground soil, so you do not want to have to crawl into your beds to reach all the plants. If you restrict the beds to four feet in width, you will be able to reach the center of the beds from both sides.

Prepping your Site

The decisions about the shape and size of your beds have been taken, so now you can continue to prepare this site. The amount of prep needed depends on how deep you are going to make your beds and which plants you want to grow in them.

For most vegetables, you will only need six inches of soil depth to keep them happily growing. Start by placing layers of newspaper, cardboard, or landscape fabric on top of the ground soil of the site you chose. Continue to pile the soil with its amendments on top. If you want to provide more room for those roots that like to grow deeper, first dig out all the existing sods. Now loosen the ground soil to a depth of around twelve inches with your garden fork or shovel. Then go ahead with your mixture of fertile soil and compost.

Planning and Locating Your Raised Bed Garden

One of the central premises of raised beds is that you do not stand on the soil and that you can reach any point in the raised bed from the outside. Therefore, your first consideration when building a raised bed is to consider how far you can reach. Typically, a raised bed will be no more than four feet wide, which assumes a comfortable reach of two feet. The length of your raised bed will vary depending on how you are planning to set out the beds.

Planning Your Raised Beds

Once you have the best layout for your raised beds, you then need to calculate the materials that you need. As your diagram is to scale, it is effortless because you can measure the sizes of the raised bed and calculate the required wood/bricks from that. You can even work out the volume of soil needed by multiplying together the length, width, and height needed of the soil. So, if your bed was 4' x 6' and you wanted the soil 1' deep, then your calculation would be 4 x 6 x 1 or 24 cubic feet of soil.

Where to Plant

You must match the right plants with the right position on the raised bed. If your garden is a small one, you might not have enough options to make do with as regards space, but there are a variety of plants that can suit different aspects and portions of the garden – be it the shady area or the damp environment or even dry soil. All you have to is to locate the best plant that will fit into the particular space.

Shady Corners of your garden

Plants, in general, require sunlight for their metabolism and production of food. It is also necessary that they get enough of it to grow. If your little garden is located in such an environment that it receives little or no sunlight, then you don't have to despair. There are other plant options you can plant in those spaces. Some plants are shade loving. You can utilize them for this space. Some of these plants include leafy crops such as cabbage, spinach, and summer salads. All of these plants prefer a cold environment, so shades are going for them.

Observe the light trajectory

Before constructing a raised bed, one of such things that I put into consideration in the direction of the sunlight and how space accommodates it, this is necessary, particularly in small gardens that fall in between walls. Note that some plants that are still growing can grow out of the sunlight once they have reached a certain height. Also, taller plants can suddenly block an area and hinder its reception of the sun.

You should make a study of your compound and find out where the sunlight rests most time of the day. Raised beds that are constructed in such spaces will naturally be warmer and sunnier because of the constant sunlight they are receiving. This is ideal because each raised bed should receive as much sunlight as possible.

To let in more light into the garden, you can cut back overhanging and overgrown vegetation and branches. If you have neighbors who have trees in their gardens that have overgrown and have started affecting the light reception in your garden, you ask them to trim it down a little for your sake. Sometimes the height of your fence can also pose a challenge to the reception of sunlight. You can reduce it to allow more sunlight, although this can cost you some of your privacy.

Providing Shelter from Elemental Forces

Plants, too, need some form of shelter and protection from the elements. When plants are exposed to too much wind, you will notice that they decimate and begin to fall off because it causes plants to dry off, and it sucks moisture off the ground.

Plants hardly get pollinated in strong winds because most insects that facilitate pollination cannot withstand the strong winds. Whenever I am planting vegetables, I try to provide them with enough protection from the wind. I surround them with hedges, walls and fences to keep the winds out. I have discovered that the best kind of windbreakers is hedges, but it is semi-permeable, being that it allows some form of wind circulation.

The other form of windbreakers such as fences can totally prevent wind from getting to the plants, but they can sometimes be dangerous in that excessively strong winds can buffer along the top edge and drop down onto the raised bed with extra force.

When to Plant?

Some plants thrive in cold weather; broccoli, for example, but tomatoes will die out in such cold temperatures. With each plant, there are the best times to plant them. You must do your research and put down frost dates and take note of soil temperatures. Under no condition should you grow any plant that is averse to cold when the frost hasn't passed?

As some plants are opposed to low temperatures, so are others that can't survive in extreme temperatures. Be careful to figure out what your garden choices may require. On average, most plants do well in reasonable soil temperatures of between sixty to seventy degrees Fahrenheit. In the event where you embark on transplanting, you must do so when temperatures are average, and the weather is just right. In the case where you transplant and the weather turns out to be harsh, then you'll have to cover them up and shield them from intense sunlight and dry winds.

Site Preparation

One of the questions most frequently asked about raised beds for growing vegetables is just how tall they should be. There is no definite answer to this question, I am afraid. There is no 'ideal height'; it is entirely up to the individual. However, there are specific considerations that you must keep in mind. These include the soil conditions under the beds, the costs involved, the depth of the soil required for your specific crop, and, of course, which height would allow you to work comfortably in your raised beds. This last aspect should take priority if you are a mature gardener.

Preparation of the Ground

Double Dig

Although the plants in your raised beds will be provided with their rich soil, some of them may grow roots that extend into the soil underneath the beds to search for additional nutrients and moisture. Therefore, it is vital to prepare the soil below by double digging it. This must be done before you start on your raised beds, and once done, need not be repeated.

Double digging simply means the depth to which you have to dig up the soil; it is approximately twenty-four inches deep, or in other words, two lengths of the blade of your shovel. Remove all the hard rocks and debris that could obstruct roots from growing down into the ground. Keep your eyes open for other large roots entering into this space. For instance, trees that grow nearby can send their roots to more than fifty feet diagonally underneath the surface, searching for nutrients and water. Double digging will provide an extensive reservoir of water and nutrients, which your plants' sturdier, deeper roots can have access to.

Digging up the ground also allows you to have a closer look at the status of the underlying soil, and to decide which amendments should be made. If it resembles clay, for instance, peat should be used to lighten it to aerate it and improve the drainage.

Improving the Subsoil

You have cleared the ground area of debris and rock and finished your double digging. If needed, you can now add some peat moss that will lighten your soil. Because peat has an acidic nature, you have to balance the pH level of the soil by adding lime. Sprinkle some rock phosphate over the plot and mix it in with the soil. Your ground area is now ready for the raised plant bed, so assemble the frames and fill up with fertile soil. When you almost reach the top of the raised bed, add compost and fertilizer. Do not add the compost and fertilizer too long before the season to avoid early, unexpected spring rainfalls to flush them too far down into your soil.

Ideal Height for Raised Beds

Consider Drainage

Raised beds have an aesthetic appeal, which speaks to many gardeners, but they also allow for proper drainage of the soil in which your veggies will be grown. In general, most raised beds are eleven inches tall, which is equal to that of two 2 by 6 standard boards. (In fact, the measurements are 1.5 by 5.5 inches.) The reason why this height is most popular is that it provides adequate drainage for the majority of crops. The best results can be achieved if you allow for another twelve inches at least of fertile soil underneath your raised bed. That will give your veggie plants up to twenty inches of good soil. Remember that raised beds usually end up not filled to the brim with soil; after every watering, the soil will compress somewhat. You will need this extra space later to add some mulch.

Consider Bending Down

Young gardeners who are fit and energetic might not even waste time thinking about this aspect since going on your knees or bending down to attend to your plants is easy, and you take it in your stride. People who suffer from backache or strain or those whose mobility has been impaired will need higher raised beds to help lighten their gardening chores. Beds can be in a range of eight to twenty-four inches high. You will quickly notice the considerable difference between tending these various beds. Taller beds are just so much more comfortable when you have to set in transplants, till the soil, weed, and harvest. It is not necessary to put extras strain on your back at all.

Cross Supports for Taller Beds

It is commonsense that taller beds will hold more volume, so you have to keep this in mind when you construct a raised bed that is taller than twelve inches (especially if it is longer than five feet). As mentioned before, after a few watering, the soil will compact slightly, becoming heavier, and the pressure may well cause your beds to bulge out on the sides in mid-span. So, for beds of this height, you will require cross supports. Place them in the middle of the span, right across the width. This will prevent the two sides from bulging out. If you purchased your raised beds from a garden center, these supports were probably included in the package, but if your raised beds are home-made, you will have to make your own using composite plastic, aluminum, or wood.

Build Up Rich Soil

The quality of your soil is by far the most important contributing factor to productivity. All the expert gardeners agree on this. Therefore, to start, you need deep soil, rich in organic matter to encourage extensive, healthy root systems that are then able to get to all the water and nutrients. A healthy root system in the soil will result in boosted productive plant growth outside the soil.

Prepare the soil

A healthy soil helps provide better nutrients to the plants. Better nutrients mean better health. Never treat your soil with chemicals if you want to grow an organic garden. Chemicals can harm you and your plants.

The first thing you need to do is get your soil tested. You may get a home testing kit or send a sample directly to a local agricultural office. When you get your soil tested, you would know the breakdown of the nutrient levels of the soil. You will also get recommendations from the experts on how to treat your soil without chemicals better.

<u>Good compost</u>

Any garden can benefit from compost. And you can make your own. One benefit of compost is it will keep your crops healthy.

Here's how to make your compost:

Get at least three feet of square space in your garden for your compost. Add leaves and garden trimmings with layers of soil in between. Apply them alternately.

Use natural fertilizers. This is crucial. Using natural fertilizers can make the soil healthier. You get better fruits and vegetables with natural fertilizers. Add a little water to keep the compost moist. Top it off with up to six inches of soil.

Buy the right plants

This is an essential step. Make sure the plants or crops you grow in your organic garden are the right ones. You need to choose the right plants that will grow in your soil. You also need to consider your climate. If it's the colder months, do not buy crops that don't grow in the cold season. If you don't know which crops grow in the hotter or colder months, you may want to check with The US Department of Agriculture or your fellow farmers. For sure, they will be glad to assist you.

Water them properly. Plants need water to survive. You must know when to water them to keep them alive and healthy. Mornings are the best time to water your plants. Avoid watering your plants at night as it is more likely to be damaged by a lot of bacteria.

Protect your plants. To avoid pests, make sure your plants get proper sunlight, moisture, and nutrients. Plants need at least six hours of full sun.

Choose the Right Location

You must choose the right spot. You want to expose your plants to sunlight because sunlight is right for them. It will help them grow and carry out the process of photosynthesis. This also means that you will be able to grow plants a lot faster, regardless of what you intend to grow. Your plants must get at least 6 hours of full sunlight. This will also help get rid of pests, insects, and certain diseases/infections.

Consider the sun, wind, water, and drainage in choosing the perfect site for your raised bed garden. It is ideal for building your raised bed garden where it gets full exposure from the sun. It is because most vegetables and flowers need at least six to eight hours of direct exposure to the sun for them to grow correctly. At the same time, it has to be located in an area near your home and near a water source. As for the drainage, some drainage problems can be resolved over time, but it is not recommended to build a raised bed garden on an area that has poor drainage.

CHAPTER 2:

Common Mistakes in raised beds gardening

Overwatering Your Plants

This is the last chance there is to reinforce the idea that your plants should be too dry than too wet. While plants need plenty of water, too much water is the deadliest thing of all. It gets into the soil around the roots and prevents them from sucking in oxygen. The roots will blacken and die. They go from having a solid texture, almost like a piece of string, and instead start to feel slimy and gross. This is all happening under the soil, though, so the first sign that most gardeners see is when the leaves of their plants start to go mushy as they rot from the inside, and if you aren't regularly checking your plants, you might not see it until the whole plant has started rotting. If you notice this early on the lowest leaves, you might be able to save the plant by digging it out to remove the rotted roots, but more often than not, it is already too late.

Not Weeding Pathways

The more significant issue with weeds is when they infest our raised bed gardens. But we shouldn't ignore their presence in and around our raised bed gardens. When we do, we are merely inviting the inevitable to happen. We're only a stiff breeze away from a seed being carried up and into the garden bed. You should always weed the pathways around and between your raised beds to reduce the presence of weeds. Reducing their presence will likewise lessen the likelihood of infestation, plus it will leave your gardens looking much more beautiful.

Not Preparing for Winter

Raised garden beds need to be protected for the winter. Many gardeners ignore this step, both with their raised beds or with flower beds directly in the ground. Then, come next spring, they wonder why their soil is such low quality. This shouldn't be a surprise, but it seems many beginners don't realize that they need to prepare for the winter the same way that the birds and bears do. The soil needs to be kept safe from the elements.

Poisoning the Growing Environment

This one ties in directly with using unsafe materials. One of the reasons that raised bed gardening is so attractive is the level of control it gives gardeners over the growing environment. While the soil in your backyard might not be healthy at all, you take control of the soil you use in your raised bed garden so that you know it is perfectly safe and healthy. However, there are many ways in which careless gardeners may poison this soil or even the environment around the raised bed garden itself. One example of this would be to use railway ties, but the material used to make the raised bed frame is only one method of poisoning the environment.

Using the Wrong Material

There are plenty of safe materials that you can use, like concrete, stone, bricks, hardwoods, and more. But there are also materials which degrade the quality of the land and the soil. Tires might be an easy way to add some circular imagery to your landscaping, but they should only be used for non-edible flowers since they could seep heavy metals into the soil. Then there are downright toxic materials like railway ties, which are so toxic to the land around them that there have been several governments issued warnings against their use in the United States. It is essential to make sure that the material you are using isn't going to end up taking a bite out of your or your plants' health.

Building Raised Beds Too Close Together

This pairs well with not making your raised garden beds too wide. If you are going to be placing garden beds next to each other, then you should make sure there are two feet or so between them. You might be able to get away with a foot and a half, but it is better to have a little more space than not enough. The reason we don't make our raised garden beds more than four feet wide is so that we can access all of our plants to keep an eye on them and maintain their health. This is the same reason that you want to have enough space to be able to maneuver between your beds easily. If you can't properly move around the garden bed, then you are effectively cutting off access to an entire side and reducing your ability to look after those far away from plants properly.

Making Your Raised Beds Too Wide

Your raised garden beds, or even those beds in the ground themselves, should never be more than four feet wide. This is done so that you can tend to all of the plants in the bed, including those in the middle that are the hardest to reach. You may believe that you can reach a little further than that and so might make an appropriately raised garden bed, but you will find that once your plants start to come in, it gets a lot harder to reach those middle ones than you expected. While they are seeds or seedlings, nothing is obstructing your view or reach, but once foliage starts to grow in, it can become like trying to navigate through a miniature jungle.

Using the Wrong Soil

You need to do your research on what you are going to grow to see if this soil mixture will work for them. Typically, most of what you want to grow are either going to enjoy this, or it will want something with a little more of a sandy texture. More minerals in the soil will increase the speed of drainage, but not every plant enjoys a sandy soil.

Ignoring the Drainage

When you mix up your soil, you are doing it to create a quickly draining texture. Raised garden beds drain better due to their elevated positions, but you still need to use well-draining soil. Introducing too many plants will block up the soil and slow down the draining while preventing anyone plant from getting enough nutrients. Weeds will also slow down the drainage. But the biggest problem is failing to include drainage holes in the raised bed frame itself. Depending on the material used, water will have a more natural or harder time getting out even with a drainage hole. You need to balance this all when building and mixing soil. Many beginners only take into account their soil or their drainage holes and not the whole spectrum of influence.

Skipping Out on Maintenance

This is another one of those mistakes that happen often enough to be embarrassing. There is simply no excuse for leaving your garden entirely untended. When you do this, you are choosing to completely ignore any signs of danger that you might have been able to catch early. If you left your house for a vacation, you would lock the front door. When you stop maintaining your raised garden beds, you are leaving them with their door wide open for pests, weeds, critters, and disease.

CHAPTER 3:

Sustainable and inexpensive materials that won't' rot

What's the Best Material for Your Raised Garden Bed's Frame?

Stone

Stone can be an excellent material to build a raised garden bed out of. It is expensive as can be from the store, but if you can find it locally or have some on your property, then you could use this. You will need to purchase mortar to fill in the gaps, keep it all together, and block weeds' entry to the bed. These beds can cost a lot of money to make, but once they are built, they can last forever. We still have stone walls from ancient history all over the world. This makes money worth it, but consider it carefully because removing it will be a lot of work.

Brick

Brick walls are another option that lasts forever and also uses mortar, so it makes sense to cover them together. Brick walls are pretty much like stone walls except that where stone walls accentuate the natural aesthetics of a yard, brick walls disrupt it. This can fit perfectly into many different styles of raised garden beds and landscaping designs, but that is the primary difference between the two. However, brick can often be more expensive than stone, so people will purchase old concrete blocks and treat them as if they were bricks.

Railroad Ties

Railroad ties are a popular choice for a recycled material that creates a feeling of American heritage, like something right out of a Norman Rockwell painting. They look great in the garden. But unfortunately, they're also a wrong choice that should be avoided at all costs. Railroad ties are treated with more chemicals than you could imagine, and a whole whack of them makes you sick. Worse than heavy metals, these ruin the soil around them, and so they shouldn't even be used for flower beds. They're a thousand times worse than tires, and the EPA has even warned about the dangers of gardeners using them.

Shipping Pallets

You find shipping pallets used in a lot of raised gardens because they are a cheap material to purchase second hand. However, you don't know what they were used to transport and pallets more than fifteen years old may have been treated with harmful chemicals. If you can find out what they were used for and when they were made then shipping pallets may still be a good fit, but if you can't find out this information, then it is best to avoid them rather than risk both the health of the soil around them as well as your own.

Cedar

Cedar, as well as redwood, is a durable wood that lasts a long time. They don't rot very quickly; they don't hold in a lot of moisture, and they aren't even appealing to most pests. They look quite striking and accentuate the natural elements of a yard, but since they are wood, they do rot. You can expect a good half-decade out of them, but they will need to be replaced over time.

Different Materials to Build Your Raised Bed

Wood or Scaffolding Boards

If you have existing wood in your garden that you are thinking of using for your raised bed, it's worth considering testing the wood to see if it has been treated with CCA. The continued migration of the arsenic into your plot, even if you are not using the wood in your raised bed, will affect the whole area eventually, migrating into your fertile soil for your crops.

Pinewood is another alternative, and the attraction is the cost, which is much lower than say redwood or cedar; however, it will not last as long as such hardy woods. But it's easy to source and easy to manage too.

Cedar, redwood, Juniper, and Yew are all naturally rot-resistant and extremely durable and long-lasting and do give a great look and finish to your garden if your budget allows. There is a reason many choose these types of wood and find them superior, their durability and versatility, as well as their aesthetic and the fact they are easy to work with. The downside is the cost is usually twice the price of say pine; also, they are not very sustainable as hardwoods are slower growers.

When visiting your lumberyard, it's a great practice to note what sizes the lumber comes in; that way, you can tailor your raised bed to this exact size minimizing any waste cuts. 8-foot lengths by 4-foot widths are a perfect size for me, but this may not work for you.

Wooden Frame Kits

Some will be reading this thinking how lazy can you be, but some people just don't have the time and ability to source materials to self build; you can find these at a lot of hardware or garden stores and, of course, Amazon. They are pre-made garden bed kits that come in a variety of sizes, are well priced, and easy to construct. Also, once built and filled, you may find because of poor durability and strength, you may see some bowing under the strain of the moist earth. Indeed, if it's starting to bow at that point, rest assured on the first torrential downpour, it will worsen. Not all are built this way, though, so if this is the option you want, have a good hunt around and look at reviews, *etc.* to make sure it is right for your project.

Brick Built Raised Beds

These can be time-consuming and require some skill to build; however, they are built to last and will serve you well for years to come, plus if built well, they look stunning in your garden.

You will need a string, a spirit level (use it at every given opportunity to get perfectly level walls!) bricks, and a hard-core base of rubble. Don't forget to leave regular gaps between brick joints to allow room for drainage; you can go ahead at the end to cover these holes with mesh to stop any clogging.

Another alternative to brick is to use blocks or concrete panels, which will require rendering to give a polished finish; these methods provide highly significant insulation for your plants at a reasonably low cost too.

The downside, though, is if you needed to move your bed, it would be troublesome to relocate. Also, you may find over time; it could crack or sink.

Railway Sleeper Raised Beds

A trendy choice is to use old rustic looking railway sleepers which give a great aesthetic to any garden, however most authentic or vintage ones will have been treated with tar and creosote, which will inevitably be transferred into your nutrient-rich soil and affect the quality of your crops.

They can be pricey to purchase, although if you hunt around, you can find a good deal at salvage yards, also not all are the same size, so some adaptation will be required to get the sizing right for your raised bed.

CHAPTER 4:

How to build your own Raised Bed Garden

Designs of Raised Bed Gardening

Few designs of raised bed gardening are as under:

Built-in Raised Beds

This design involves raising plants in compost, which is higher than the surface. Most generally, this can be achieved with any sort of cage or frame built from timber, stone, or even hay bales or repurposed material such as old dressers.

The beds raised may be as modest or imaginative as you wish. A raised bed planter may be a permanent feature for bringing in and maturing annual plants. The actual cost of putting up the raised bed would rely on how complex you render it, but once built, raised beds are far more costly than conventional gardens to manage. They have a lot of advantages.

You should put it where the sun or shadow is the greatest for the plants you want to grow when you create a raised bed instead of heading in-ground.

You will also prevent the decimation of your plants by tunneling rodents. In a raised bed, plants will be safer and more efficient, because you can monitor the consistency of the soil and water runoff.

If you create the sides large enough to make a bench, you would also be able to sit down and plant, which makes it harder for someone with back issues to tend the seeds.

Sheet Metal Raised Beds

Another significant benefit of the elevated bed garden is that they rest just above the underground freeze line, and the soil gets colder in the morning, so you can start planting earlier. Steel must ensure the soil absorbs surface heat from the air.

Sheet metal allows the forms simpler to mold. Often, supplying the heat required to develop Mediterranean plants like sage and lavender is a perfect way to.

Square Foot Raised Beds

Square Foot planting means splitting the growing area into tiny square parts, usually one foot per segment. The goal is to create an intensively planted vegetable garden or kitchen garden that is highly efficient. Use a raised bed to grow vegetables helps you to monitor the consistency of the soil to protect it from compacting. The roots of vegetables can grow unimpeded. The beds needn't be far off the ground to get the benefits of living in an elevated room. Just 6 to 8 inches can suffice. Those garden beds are necessary to increase the drainage of the soil.

Herb Spiral

Spiral gardens is a common permaculture technique, as this herb garden at Mill Creek Gardens. They are increasing the amount of available planting area in your garden without taking up any field space. You may quickly create them from mortar, concrete, wood, or even dig the soil up. The odd plant form and swirl give your garden an eye-grabbing focal point. Herbs are the plants of preference in this picture, but the spiral nature helps you to grow something.

Hoop House Raised Bed

You can build a multi-seasonal vegetable garden with a little pre-planning. Raised beds allow you greater freedom in managing your garden's growing conditions and make it harder for animals to get to your vegetables. When you're constructing a hoop house on top of a raised bed, you can get ready for whatever season, tackle snow, and give yourself a spring head start.

Raised Bed Border

Lifted beds are a perfect choice for steep sloping yards. You may establish the appearance of a level garden by raising the beds at their lowest points like those stone raised beds. Make your beds large enough that you can always have a layered flower garden with a border of shrubs lining the back of the garden and plenty of space for perennials that will provide colors, textures, and edge-softening drapes.

Trough Bed Gardens

Use animal feeding troughs is the best way to build constructed bed gardens. There is no need for installation, so make careful to drill any drainage holes in the bottom before applying the dirt. The metal brings a modern feel to the greenhouse and conducts electricity, warming the spring soil. Depending on what you have selected to produce, during the hottest part of the summer, the plants will require some extra water.

Shallow Raised Beds

The most common and favorite among all types of raised beds are shallow raised beds, which are also popularly known as 'raised ground beds.' These are common because they are the easiest to make and the easiest to maintain. They require the least amount of effort, look great, and are easily cultivated. To make these beds, you can use any type of material, i.e., rubber, plastic, vinyl, concrete blocks, bricks, stones, or lumber – among which cedar is the most common. These beds are generally less than one foot from the ground and rectangular.

Deep Raised Beds

These raised beds are a little higher than one foot from the ground. This type of bed is normally constructed at waist-level or chest-level and specially designed for people who cannot bend or are physically challenged as in being in a wheelchair. These types of raised beds make it possible for persons with physical challenges who love gardening but cannot indulge in this wonderful hobby actually to enjoy gardening to their heart's content. These types of beds are also constructed where the topsoil is extremely poor in quality and, hence, the plants will require all the nutrients the raised bed soil can offer.

Elevated Beds

This is a separate type of raised bed. You will find these on legs or stilts that will make it look like a table. This is also called 'the standing garden.' The beds are usually shallow and made of wood. They are often used to grow seasonal or annual flowers, shallow root vegetables, and herbs.

These beds are almost always used in areas where pesky insects are found in plenty, where soil might be too ridden with various diseases, and where the gardeners cannot bend for gardening.

Terraced Raised Beds

The terraced beds are typically used on hillsides to prevent soil erosion and raise food crops. These look like steps when you look at the hillside, which allows for easy access. With terraced raised beds, you can grow any type of plant – cascading plants, vegetables, flowers, creepers – anything. All plants will look great, and gardening is relatively easy with this type of raised bed as well. In most cases, these types of raised beds are built with strong materials such as concrete, bricks, and stones. At the same time, terraced raised beds made out of wood are also trendy.

Custom-Designed Raised Beds

Gardens can suit almost any room. With a little imagination, you can build a whole sitting area of the greenhouse. It comes fitted with a lamppost and a potting shed. Attach a part of the table, like the one at the end of the front room, and you have seating for the dining area outside. This garden should take on a normal, rustic look as the plants fill in, and the forest season.

Raised Bed Arbor

Using a trellis or arbor with a raised bed allows the growing of vegetables much smoother and leaves them neater than if they were scattered on the grass. Vertical planting helps you to grow more plants without taking up more room. Whether you grow flowering vines or spreading crops, this teepee trellis garden provides a growing arbor that offers the vines plenty of exposure to sunlight without blocking the plants in the beds higher below. Through leaning two bamboo poles together, binding them together, and wrapping garden netting over, the build may be as easy as building an A-frame.

Tiered Raised Bed

There are also few restrictions on Tiered Raised Beds. This Home Stratosphere multi-level elevated bed appears like a pagoda or a pool. You could not even see the elegant wood frame that holds them until the flowers spread out. It looks fantastic throughout the entire year. You may also decorate it with festive greens and lights throughout the holidays to make it look like a Christmas tree.

Raised bed garden layout

a) Choose a bright location, if necessary, find beds away from trees and hedge.

b) Create beds 4' (1.2 m) long or less.

c) Provide room between beds for cycling, mowing, or moving with a wheelbarrow. Mine are 20" (51 cm) long.

d) Using a rectangular bed grid form. That encourages exposure. If you live in a cold-weather zone with constant freezing temperatures, you can build or buy a garden bed system with a cover to keep frost off the soil and the new seedlings. All you will need to construct is a simple frame to cover the bed like a tent with heavy transparent plastic material. The one below is constructed with PVC and wood for the frame. You can easily make them smaller to fit over a single raised bed.

Steps to Build A Raised Bed

1. Measure and Cut Lumber

2. Pick Frame Orientation

3. Mark and Drill Pilot Holes

4. Attach with Screws

5. Attach Corner or angles Brackets for Added Power (Optional)

Measure and Cut Lumber

Depending on the size of your raised bed along with the dimensions Timber you purchase, you might not have to generate any cuts, but generally, timber will have to get cut. Some construction supply shops will make these reductions for you. I've three 5x10 foot raised beds constructed from 2x12 timber. I purchased the timber in 10-foot lengths; therefore, three boards were required for every framework. Just one 10-foot plank has been cut in half to every bed.

Pick Frame Orientation.

Decide if you need the bed to be marginally more, Drive screws through the 5-foot finish planks to the endings of the 10-foot boards), marginally broader, Drive

Screws through the 10-foot boards to the ends of the 5-foot finish planks), or split the difference, begin at one corner, and then lap every plank towards the conclusion of the following board).

Mark and Drill Pilot Holes

Most timber framing is done only with nails and hammer, but screws using pre-drilled pilot holes have been used alternatively, the framework will fit tighter, continue longer, twist less, and can help prevent the boards from dividing. Begin by indicating the diameter of the board on each end, which is to be drilled (which means it's possible to drill holes near the middle of the plank. Use a drill bit that's slightly narrower than the screws you intend on using. A 1/8th inch drill bit is suggested for #10 screws at softwood. Drill the pilot hole through the surface of a single plank and throughout the conclusion of another board.

Merge Frame with Screws

Be sure to use screws that are long enough to maintain the boards together for several decades. A two-inch screw may hold a 2x4 board to get a minimal time; however, the twist thread, is #10 twist that's 3.5 inches long and should Hold for several decades. After drilling the pilot holes, then begin the screws and allow Them to stretch about a quarter inch from every hole on the opposite side of the plank. That means you'll have the ability to feel if the screws inserted into the pockets on another board. Hold the 2 boards close together and while every screw is tightened.

Attach Corner or Angles Mounts for extra strength

There are Various Kinds of angles and corner mounts Ranging from approximately 50 cents to $15, which can add strength to the corners. Some are so powerful, they'd maintain the bed frame together without added screws, but the better ones are costly and need bolts to maintain the angles into the framework. If you assembled the framework correctly, with great exterior screws, then the framework will last for many decades with no further support.

Measures to Level and Square the Raised Bed Frame

1. Place Raised Bed Frame Close into the Closing Site

2. Square the Bed Frame

3. Utilize Level to Determine High and Low Locations

4. Dig High Spots Away and Fill Low Locations

5. Closing Check Frame for Square and Level

6. Backfill around Bed Frame with Soil or Gravel.

CHAPTER 5:

Best vegetables to plant in a raised bed

Types of vegetables

There are a lot of vegetables you can grow in a raised bed; in fact, you can grow almost anything you want. Here is more information about the many different vegetables and how they will grow in raised beds.

Root Vegetables

Root vegetables such as carrots, beets, parsnips, radishes, and so on do well in raised beds. Carrots and parsnips grow deep roots, so you either need an eight to twelve-inch-deep raised bed or you need to have dug down into the soil below to give them the space they need to grow. The deeper root vegetables will not work if you have a shallow bed and either poor soil beneath it or a wire mesh to prevent burrowing pests. Raise your beds higher (12" is fine) to grow deep-rooted veg if the soil below is poor. Because raised beds tend to be free of rocks, you end up with good quality carrots and parsnips with long, well-formed roots. Add horticultural sand to your raised beds to make it drain better, so your carrots grow straighter. Potatoes, though, aren't particularly suited to raised beds. In smaller beds, they will grow down into the soil beneath and require a lot of digging to get out. In larger beds, you are practically going to have to empty the bed to get all the potatoes out. It is a personal preference, and some people will plant potatoes in raised beds, but I prefer to grow them in bags and then use the spent compost in the beds the following year. The advantage of growing in bags is that you don't find potato plants appearing in your raised beds the following year, and nor do you have to do a lot of digging to get them out of the ground. If you do want to grow potatoes in a raised bed, then you need your soil to be 18–24 inches deep and be able to mound up the earth around the shoots as they grow. They will do well in a raised bed because they need a loose, free-draining soil, which is one of the main premises behind raised beds. You will also get a good-sized crop of potatoes, but my personal preference is to avoid it because of the digging involved … it is far easy just to empty a bag! Plus, for years afterward, you will be finding potatoes growing in the bed, which will disturb your other vegetable crops.

Leafy Greens

Most leafy greens such as kale, spinach, cauliflower, lettuce, and so on do fantastically in a raised bed. Many of these can be started early in the year, and some, such as kale, pak choi, cauliflower, broccoli, and others, can be started soon in the year and overwintered. Because raised beds warm faster than the surrounding soil, you can often get a good harvest before summer and they will do very well because they like free-draining soil.

Be aware that these will get eaten by pests, particularly slugs, snails, and caterpillars. A tight mesh cage built over the bed will keep the caterpillars off and may prevent larger slugs and snails. You will still need to keep an eye on the plants and act against any slugs that find their way into your raised bed. Young plants are at risk of damage from birds, so also need covering. I will often use a plastic polytunnel for the young plants as they benefit from the extra warmth as well as the protection from birds.

Onions, Leeks, and Garlic

Any member of the onion family does well in a raised bed because they like plenty of organic matter and free-draining soil. They do tend to have a long growing season (grown from seed they can take over 100-day s to mature) and raised beds to ensure that you can get planting early in the year.

The onion family does not like competition, nor do they like drying out. Make sure you keep the weeds down because they will crowd out the onions. In hot weather, water these beds regularly because if they dry out too much, the plants will end up dying, and the bulbs will not form properly.

Tomatoes

Tomatoes are greedy feeders and, if you add extra compost to your raised bed, then they will do very well indeed. However, the only issue comes with staking the tomatoes as the stakes are not secure in the loose soil. You can either drive the stakes into the firm soil below your raised bed or fix them to the edges of the bed. I have screwed wooden trellises to the raised bed as support for plants, which worked very well.

Tomatoes ripen with heat rather than just sun, so you may find that you need to fleece your tomato bed to give them some extra warmth, particularly towards the end of the growing season. You can wrap clear plastic over the bed or create a polythene polytunnel to keep them warm, so they produce a good crop.

Peas and Beans

These will do very well in raised beds though you may have issues with supporting taller crops such as runner beans. Driving supports into the soil beneath your bed, or fixing them to the bed itself will help.

Young plants are at risk of damage from birds, so they will need covering and protecting. With beans, you will need to build a frame from bamboo canes, using ten to twelve-foot-high canes for them to climb up. Either lash short canes to these or build a frame of garden twine to help encourage the beans to spread and climb up.

Peas also need support, and traditionally pea sticks are used. These are dead branches or specially bought pea sticks. Alternatively, you can build a mesh from garden twine, and the pea plants will use those for support. You can also buy special pea netting, which the plants will climb up. Putting a six-foot bamboo cane in each corner, plus one in the middle will allow you to build a mesh of twine that will support your peas. Add extra canes as necessary, depending on the size of your raised bed.

Vine Crops

These are not very well suited for raised beds, mainly as squashes are very greedy feeders indeed. The problem with long trailing vines is you run out of space, and they can crowd out neighboring plants. You can build supports for them, and you can grow your cucumbers vertically, which will help reduce the space requirements.

Courgettes (zucchini) are available in bush forms which do not take up as much space as the following forms and are well suited for raised beds. Other squash plants, such as pattypan squashes, are reasonably compact plants which makes them suitable for a raised bed.

Plants such as pumpkins are generally very rambling and are going to take up vast amounts of space. They will not be contained within a raised bed and will expand outside of their designated area, taking over your vegetable plot.

With the long, trailing vines, you can build a small raised bed to plant them in. This is a variation on the hill method, where the soil is very nutrient-rich to give the plant a good start in life.

Because squashes such as pumpkins and butternut squashes grow so big, you should avoid growing them in a raised bed because they are going to grow like crazy and crowd out all your other plants. Although you can grow these large plants vertically, they will still take up a lot of space, and you will have to grow varieties that produce smaller fruits.

What not to Grow

Soft fruit bushes such as raspberries, blackberries, and so on are not suited to raised beds because of the space they take up. It is far more cost-effective to put them in the ground, unless your soil is not suitable for them, in which case use free-standing containers. You can use raised beds for them, but most people will not, preferring to use the space for vegetables.

Autumn fruiting raspberries should always be grown in containers because they propagate by sending out runners. These are incredibly invasive and will get everywhere. I found them growing through the path and invading neighboring plots when I uncovered them on one of my allotments.

Strawberries, though, are well suited to a raised bed but are best grown in a two or three-layer planter to maximize your use of space. There are plans online for multi-layered planters that you can build, which allow you to grow a lot of strawberries in a small area.

Other permanent plants such as rhubarb are also not suited for raised beds, purely because they are taking up valuable space that could be used for something else. I inherited a bed with rhubarb plants in, and the entire bed (as you can see) is taken up by two plants. These are going to be moved at the end of the growing season to be planted directly into the soil. The raised bed will be used for growing annual crops and put into the crop rotation schedule.

Asparagus is another permanent crop that doesn't need to go in a raised bed. However, as they do like to be planted quite deep, you can grow them in a raised bed, planting them at the bottom of it and then building up the ideal soil for them. It's easier in some cases than digging trenches to plant the asparagus crowns in.

Benefits of growing vegetables

Did you realize that raised garden beds are simpler for you? When you use a raised garden bed, it is simpler for your back and knees. You can invest your energy working in your garden and not stress over hurting soon.

Better for Drainage

Raised vegetable garden beds have better drainage, and this implies plants aren't exposed to a lot of water when it rains. Since one of my errors as a beginner gardener was to over water, I felt this was a superior method to support my plants.

Likewise, since we get those monster rainstorms, we love such a great amount during hot days, I felt that having a better drainage system for my garden was gainful.

Easier to Build Soil

The reason I didn't begin my garden on the ground was that I felt that it would be too much work. It is much simpler to include soil up than working changes into the ground.

Simple to Build

Building raised vegetable garden beds are extremely simple. You can make this into a one-day DYI project. Even your children can help to build their garden raised bed!

All you must assemble your raised vegetable garden beds are some accessible devices and material and obviously, an additional pair of hands.

CHAPTER 6:

Defend your garden by animals

Attract good guys

Predatory mites and ladybugs can get rid of pests. Knowing how to manage insects will help you get rid of other pests. You can attract predators to the garden by planting certain plants and flowers or using commercially available attractions. Garden predators eat pests, but they don't just eat pests. They will move around your neighborhood and go out if you provide them with your favorite floral food, some of which can be grown as edible or ornamental. Sweet clover, white alder, nasturtium, strawberry, fennel, dill, cow, coriander, morning glory, and cumin are all on account of good bugs. Bring benefits. Many ornamental eats, like this nasturtium, give pollen and nectar to predatory insects.

Snails and slugs

Servants look just as awful as they act. They are vicious, intimate, and absolutely without social qualities. They eat almost everything in the garden where they can go, leaving a sticky trail to tell you who is responsible for the butcher shop.

Control. Snails and slugs (snails rich enough to have a mobile home), to keep their nature moist and slender, look for dark and humid places, work at night, or indoors. Like vampires, they avoid sunlight and heat. Because they move slowly, snails and slugs are easy to catch as long as you can find them. At night, go hunting with a flashlight or setting traps: planks or stones placed on the ground where creatures can hide.

Snails aren't exactly fun to grab, but they can get stuck at the end of an ice cream stick or something. Whatever you do, put them in a box of soap or saltwater. Instead, you can kill them and sprinkle them with a little salt or wood ash.

Ladybugs

Bones, also known as beetles, live to shiny tits on my list of favorite creatures. They're cute, and I'm stupid for the cute ones. But ladies are more than that and acquire all the good vibes I send them. Ladies eat aphids; Every mistake eaten by ears is a friend of the gardener. They also eat powdery mildew, mites, bumps, potato larvae in Colorado, and other soft-bodied insects.

They are oval, dark brown with orange spots, and covered with hairs. They, like their parents, eat aphids and the like. Learn to recognize this gardening friend and protect him when you see him.

Mantises

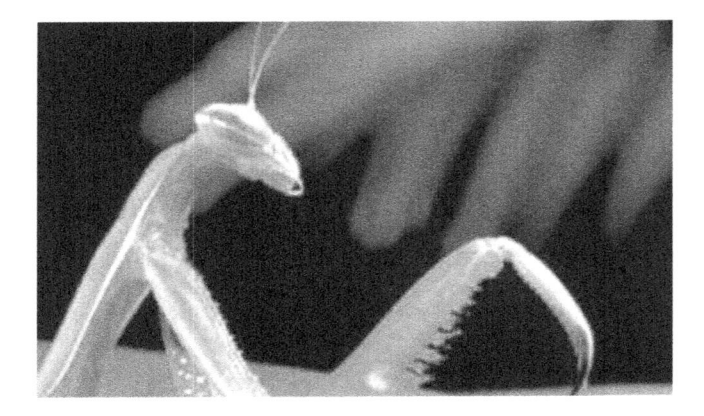

The mantis is often considered a poster of beneficial insects, nonetheless.

Size and aggressive appearance are not as useful in the garden as a bunch of ladybugs or larvae of green lace. Yet they eat pests (although they do eat both boons and pollinators if they can catch them) and it's fun to watch them.

This susceptible creature doesn't look exactly like a parasite killer. And it's not, at least not in the adult stage. But when the green lace enters the practical telephone booth and goes into its Superbug larva, watch out for all the aphids and stems, mites and turtledoves, all of you, chewing soft-bodied plants. Lion ears are free! Adults with green wings also feed on the nectar of certain flowers. There are other benefits, but none are as evident and colorful as these. If you see strange insects on your plants that the plants don't eat, you might be able to look for pests. Look for an excellent book to verify the identity of suspicious pests before making any effort to remove them.

Ecological control check

Use barriers (covered with rows of fabric, repellents, planting fragrant comrades) to avoid contact between pests and hosts. Use traps to attract pests from target plants. Manually select problematic parasites. A 15-minute morning tour of the garden is needed to keep Colorado beeches under control.

Don't go nuclear

The goal is to kill certain pests, enough that the damage they cause is not significant. This paradox is at the heart of an ecological approach to pest control. In an ecologically healthy garden, natural predators of various pests generally keep the number of these pests small enough that the damage they cause does not interfere with the growth of their plants and production. For this to happen, pests must be available at all times so that predators can eat them. Otherwise, the predators will starve or move to an environment where there is enough food like someone else's garden. Here the problem is the same as in the rest of nature: the predator population lags behind the prey population. Compared to their predators, garden pests produce younger, do so more often, and mature faster. When all predatory pests are gone and the pest returns, it can quickly establish a large and significantly destructive population before being confronted with predatory food again, in a so-called secondary epidemic.

Fence: your best defense

Our country garden has been deer-free for many years and our corn land without raccoons, thanks to an electric fence. You can run a wire (actually a plastic wire woven into small metal wires) to the deer's nose (about three feet) around the garden.

Even if you prefer an electric fence, this may not be an option in your neighborhood. Also, you may not want to place electric fences around your paved area if you just plant one or two tanks. A chicken wire high or four feet high fence will be enough to deter small creatures, but that won't keep deer away. A simple electric fence can be all that is needed to keep raccoons and deer out of your yard. Although most systems sold for home use do not provide a dangerous voltage discharge, you will probably want to show a sign to inform visitors that the fence is on.

Pest and Disease Management without Chemicals

Container plants naturally experience fewer pest attacks since they are grown in a cleaner and more regularly sanitized environment than field or garden plants. Nevertheless, it does not make them free from pests, diseases, or other issues. An insect could sneak into any garden, and fungal spores are always present in the air. Plant diseases, "weeds and pests can be a danger to crops. The only solution is to spray pesticides regularly", says "chemical companies" However, chemicals might create more issues than they resolve. Sustainable farmers align with nature to maintain soil, crops, weeds, diseases, and pest life in balance. We call this integrated pest management (IMP) or natural pest management.

Integrated pest management prevents pest problems and plant diseases, and keeps hazardous chemicals away from us and our surroundings. It as well prevents problems of pesticide resistance and chemical reliance. Even though you are to make use of pesticides, it is significant to ascertain if pests are damaging your plants, the intensity of the damage being done, and whether creatures in the garden are already taken care of the pest. After that, you can decide on if and when chemicals are to be used, and what type to use. The best method to control both diseases and pests is to ensure plants remain healthy.

Start with Prevention

• Select disease-resistant types. Many vegetables and ornamental plants have been confirmed to be resistant to diseases, like rust, mildew, and canker.

• Examine plants before buying them to ascertain they're healthy. After that, carefully clean them before planting.

• Do not over-crowd your plants. Ventilation prevents the condition of dampness that encourages the growth of fungi and other diseases.

• Take note of moisture levels if the soil is too dry or too wet to correct the situations. Ensure plant dryness all the time.

• Examine your plants. Attend to issues before getting out of hand. Take out and destroy any plants or fruit that you suspect to have contracted disease.

• Ensure you are always clean. Viruses or bacteria could be spread by your clothes, hand, and footwear. Wash your hands before and after working on your plants and wash your clothes as you might have been in contact with unhealthy plants.

• Clean your tools. Soil sticking to tools may accommodate disease organisms. Also, wash pots before you reuse them.

• Make use of clean containers and clean potting mix.

• Remove any already infected plants and those that have more than half of their leaves gone.

• Check for pest every day when you water. Remember to check on the beneath of leaves because of the hiding place for starving bugs and their eggs.

• Decide on how much you are ready to deal with it. The plan is not to eliminate the pest, but to control it.

• Understand what pest you're having an issue with. Consult your local extension service if you are not sure of the pest. Doing this will make you adopt the pest control systems specific to your issue, instead of pouring varieties of chemical on the plant in an attempt to know which work better.

• Problems with smaller pests like whiteflies or aphids, spider mites, could be harder to control and might spread plant infections. To eliminate these pests, use organic pest control

• Build healthy soil, which presents a friendly abode to insects and helps prevent numerous plant diseases.

• Plant at the right time, diseases and pests mostly respond to the climate, like the first warm day or the first rains. Consulting other farmers about these methods and observing the growth of each crop will assist you in knowing the best time to plant. Planting before the usual time will ensure crops are matured enough to resist diseases or pests that show up at a particular period. While planting, later on, could lead to the death of most diseases and pests due to no available food.

• Look for pests, observe if insects are helping or damaging your crops. Plant-eating insects are a normal part of farming. They do slight harm to crops as far as they strike a balance with other insects, particularly the ones that consume pests.

• If you still experience pest attack after all the precautions, try (IPM) Integrated Pest Management

• If you need to act, make use of simple pest control measures that are safe for your plants, you, and the environment as a whole.

• Check up your crops frequently to help you know when to permit friendly insects to perform their duty, and the need to spray with natural pesticides or other pest control methods arise. When looking for diseases and pests, ask questions like:

1. Are the plants being eaten by an insect?

2. Are friendly insects keeping pests under control?

3. Is damage to the increase? Will it affect the crop yield?

4. Is it a harmless, friend, or pest?

At times the insects you easily see are defensive to your plants by eating the pests. And the plants might be at a growth stage where they could survive pest damage and stay healthy.

Worms are essential for healthy soil. Spiders, bees, and most insects that reside in water are friends and help in controlling pests. As well, small wasps or flies with a long, thin tube at their back are friends. The ideal thing is to leave a friendly insect to help your crops.

Pests damage crops by eating them or sucking the liquid in them

Sapsuckers include mealybugs and scale insects, aphids, whiteflies, plants and leafhoppers, nematodes, mites and thrips

Plant-eating insects are snails, slugs, plant and pod borers and caterpillars

Plant Good Neighbors

When you're considering plants for containers that are going to be going into the same container, be sure that they go well together. This means that all the plants in one pot or container should require the same amount of moisture and light. If you combine plants that have different needs, they're not going to thrive together. So, if you have a plant that requires full sun, such as a tomato plant, you should choose other vegetables that will also enjoy full suns, such as pepper plants or some herbs.

To find out what a plant requires, you can check the tag if you purchase it from a nursery, check the seed packet, or go online and find more information about it.

Insect Management

In organic farming, the idea is not to eliminate insects but to manage them. An organic farmer can successfully manage insects if he knows what they need to survive, how they interact with the environment, and how they can be manipulated to protect your farm. As soon as you find out more about insects, you would be able to draft a plan and incorporate different strategies in effectively managing them to protect your crops. Getting rid of pests is essential in organic farming. Pests can also damage crops and will make you lose money. Here are some things you can do to get rid of pests without using any chemicals:

Crop rotation

Rotating crops can promote soil fertility. It can also help in getting rid of pests that can damage your crops. Crop rotation involves altering the type of crops that a farmer grows on his organic farm. When they alternate crops, the species will not get used to the type of plant that is being cultivated. Crop rotation is a lot better than using chemicals in getting rid of pests. If you have an organic farm, using chemicals is a no-no. Chemicals can damage the crops as well as the soil that is being cultivated.

Intercropping

This method will make it harder for pests to target a particular crop. Intercropping involves the simultaneous cultivation of more crops but in the same field. When you plant different varieties of crops on the same field, the distance between types increases, making it difficult for pests to stay on a particular crop or target the main crop.

CHAPTER 7:

Advantages of Gardening in raised beds

Easy to service/maintain

With a raised bed, you have the advantage of height, which means that you do not have to bend over as far to take care of your vegetables. This is particularly advantageous if you are prone to suffer from backache.

Weed-free

A raised bed is not troubled to nearly the same extent by the incursion of weeds, as all the soil/compost mix is freshly added. For any weeds that do appear, they are easier to remove as the compost mix does not compact like garden soil. It is far easier to control destructive pests within a raised bed garden. This is simply because you are off the ground, and so keeping a natural barrier up in front of creeping pests like garden slugs. With a slightly higher raised bed of around two feet, then you are not troubled quite as much with carrot fly, for instance, who tend to be low fliers. So out with backbreaking weeding tasks, along with digging over waterlogged soil and filtering out rocks and stones, in with easy gardening methods for the busy householder, and fresh vegetables for the whole family with the minimum of hassle.

Excellent Aeration

The older, traditional way to create raised beds is simply to dig up the soil, piling it into rows. You can follow this method and then support the two sides by using solid frames. Otherwise, place your frames in place and then fill them up with compost, farmyard manure mixed with quality soil. Whichever way you choose to do it, your plants will flourish in this enriched soil, and its loose structure will allow excellent air circulation around all the roots.

Good Drainage

Even during a downpour of rain, your raised beds will render good drainage—no wonder this method is so popular in the tropics with its heavy rainfall. Because the soil has such a loose texture, water will seep slowly into the bed instead of a making a quick runoff with the accompanying washing away of all fertile topsoil. Furthermore, all the excess water can quickly drain away.

The Spreading of Roots

Although plant roots can be quite persistent in their effort to grow, they will find it challenging to do so in tightly compacted soil. In loose soil, they can grow and spread out to their hearts' content. Furthermore, a framed bed will retain the moisture after watering a lot longer than the more traditionally raised beds because the frames prevent water loss on the sides of the beds more effectively. Drying out of the beds can, therefore, be prevented, and good root spreading will follow.

Minimum Risk of Compact Soil

A raised bed will not wholly deter your smaller pets like dogs and cats from digging and rolling around in your gardening soil, but it definitely will keep humans and larger pets or animals at bay. This will prevent the tamping down of the soil. The ideal width for your raised beds is three to four feet, making it easy for you to do your gardening chores such as weeding, harvesting, and fertilizing without having to step onto the beds.

Improved Weed Control

When you cultivate the soil for normal vegetable beds, you expose a lot of the weed seeds that have been lying dormant underground shielded from the sun. The exposure to sunlight and extra moisture they receive during irrigation will provide them with the opportunity to start sprouting, just what they have been waiting for. Very quickly, they will feed on the nutrient-rich soil prepared for your vegetable plants and begin to flourish.

Easier than Amending Existing Soil

The remedy for alkaline soil is to add Sulphur, for acidic soil lime can be added. Sometimes applications have to be repeated several times to get the desired effect, but a downpour can undo all your hard work in a flash. It is not a simple, straightforward process to change the intrinsic nature of any type of soil.

Garden on Top of Existing Turf

Mark your area, and then place multiple layers of cardboard and newspaper on the area. Erect your frames and then simply continue to fill them with grass clippings, soil, sand, decomposed farmyard manure, and compost. Plant your seeds or seedlings in this rich mixture, and you have started your garden without too much backbreaking labor.

Avoid Root Run from Larger Plants and Trees

Sometimes you will find that the only available space left in your garden for your vegetables is near a number of well-established trees. These trees have massively huge roots to anchor them to the ground and will devour all the nutrients in the soil, leaving very little for your vegetable plants. You may be able to get rid of some of these invasive roots, but it is an impossible task to get completely rid of them all. Using chemicals to try to kill the roots is not an option because these very same chemicals can harm or even kill your vegetable plants. However, your raised beds will be safe from this problem since tree roots generally grow downwards and will not reach into the raised beds.

More Effective Pest Control

Creepy crawlies are true to their description, they usually enter vegetable patches this way, crawling away until they find food. Encountering an obstacle like a solid frame will deter some of them from crawling up. They may just pick the more comfortable option of continuing along the ground. To protect your plants from soil parasites like nematodes, line your raised beds along the sides and the bottom with plastic. If you fear annoying rodents burrowing their way into your beds, use a netting of wire, placing it at the bases of your beds.

Extra Available Space

Raised beds in traditional fashion provide more space for plants growing along the sides of the beds. Although this advantage does not apply to framed beds, they can provide additional space in another manner. Many of the plants growing along the side edges of the frames will extend over these side edges, leaving more room for other plants on the top surface of the bed. More light will be able to reach the plants as well.

Extended Growing Season

We all know how long it takes the ground to thaw in spring, but raised beds speed up this thawing process. This means that you can start transplanting your seedlings much earlier in the season, giving them a wonderful head start. If the area where you live has a short window period to grow your edibles in the outside garden, this extra time will make a huge difference.

Intensive Gardening with Higher Yield

It is a fact that a higher yield will be obtained by growing your veggies in raised beds instead of on flat ground beds. Attributing factors are the good aeration of the soil and extensive root run, but the leading cause is the intensive nature of this kind of gardening. Raised beds allow you to plant a greater variety of different kinds of vegetables closer together than could be done on flat ground.

Solution for Mobility Challenged Gardeners

Not all gardeners are young, energetic, and healthy people. Many experienced gardeners find it difficult to continue bending down for weeding and tending their vegetable patches as they grow older and experience health challenges. Raised beds can be built or assembled to the exact width or height that will suit every individual. It can even be planned and laid out in a fashion to accommodate wheelchair users and allow them freedom of movement to plant and harvest their vegetables quickly.

Portability

If you find that your vegetable plants are not exposed to enough sunlight in their current spot, you can just move your raised bed without too much effort. Portability is one of the advantages of this method of gardening. Beds with wire bottoms can simply be dragged to a brighter location. Otherwise, dismantle the frames and then reassemble your beds in their new spots. With care, you can move the plants, as well as the soil, contend without any damage.

CHAPTER 8:

Deciding on Your Raised Bed Garden

Now that you have chosen to start your own raised bed garden, you must be pretty excited to get started. Unfortunately, getting started first means planning and deciding on the specifications of the raised beds themselves. So, it isn't time to get your hands dirty quite yet, but that doesn't mean you can't have a ton of fun with this process.

You are going to need to decide on some very important features that could entirely change the way that your raised bed garden looks, feels, and functions. These features include the size of the beds you will be raising. There is no single right answer for what size they should be; that is entirely up to you. But it is important to be aware of how size changes the function of the garden. Likewise, you are going to need to decide on what type of material to use for the bed's frame. Again, this is your choice, and so we'll be looking at all sorts of different materials to see the pros and cons of each. Finally, it is also important to choose a design. A raised garden bed doesn't just need to be a rectangle. You'll discover tons of raised bed garden designs that you can copy or use to brainstorm your own. When it comes to this step, your imagination is the limit, and that's what makes it so much fun.

Big Garden Bed or Small Garden Bed: Which is Better?

When it comes to size, we need to consider width and height primarily. Length is going to be determined by how much space is available in the garden. You could have a raised garden bed that goes on forever (if you had space). This infinite bed could produce quite well as long as it had enough height for the roots of the plants and small enough width for you to be able to check and tend to each plant. Length doesn't need to factor into considerations of size, and so we can toss any concerns about that particular variable out the window.

Left with width and height, we can start to address the question of whether it is better to be big or small. The answer to that a little complicated in that the best answer is "either." The real problem in size doesn't come from being big or being small but from being too big or too small. With size, the problem areas are on either end of the size chart (tiny or huge), but the middle section of that chart (small or big) is a perfect fit for your raised garden bed. Let's start with width.

If your raised garden bed isn't wide enough, then you may not have any space to grow your plants. It is easy to look at a garden bed with a tiny width and know that your plants won't fit and so this isn't a problem that most gardeners run into. The more common issue is to have too wide of a raised garden bed. This is the gardening equivalent of the adage, "eyes bigger than your stomach." While the equation "more room = more plants" is technically correct, what this leaves out is the fact that you are still required to tend to those plants. If there is too much space for you to reach over, then you aren't going to be able to get at the plants in the middle of a wide raised bed. This leads to mistreated plants and signs of sickness or infestation going unnoticed until it is too late. So how do we go about making sure that our raised beds aren't too wide?

The best rule of thumb is to make them no wider than four feet across if you have access to each of the sides. If you have a garden bed with a side that you can't get to, because it up against your house, for example, then you should knock a foot off that. If you go over this size, you may not have problems getting to the plants in the middle, while everything is still just a seedling. But once their foliage starts to come in and the bed fills out, suddenly is it much harder to get to those tricky-to-reach plants. Keep in mind; this number is an average based on the height and reach of most people. If you are shorter, then you should knock half a foot off your width. Taller gardeners can get away with adding a little to the width, but this could be an issue if you need to go away and get someone to watch over your garden.

Height is an easier calculation to make. The average height for a raised bed is between half a foot to three feet tall. However, as we are primarily discussing beds with a bottom, we should stick to at least a foot in height. The taller a bed is, the more soil you have added to it. The roots of your plants are going to spread out in that soil and search for nutrients. A smaller bed in half a foot range would need to use a mesh bottom to prevent critters from accessing your garden from below while also providing the roots access to the natural soil beneath. So what we need is a bed high enough that the roots don't run out of space. That's a foot at the minimum. If you are planting lots in the raised bed, then you may want to go even taller.

Going taller is going to have a few different effects. One, it is going to allow for better drainage in the bed. But it is also going to trap moisture for longer. So the water will drain away from the roots quicker, but there is much more soil to drain through, and so the bed will hold the moisture longer. This means that the taller a bed is, the less it is going to need to be watered. This is doubly good because most raised garden beds use wooden frames, and the more they are exposed to water, the quicker they will decay and need to be replaced.

Speaking of the wooden frame, it is essential to remember that the soil inside the frame will be pushing it outwards. That is, the soil doesn't just want to stay in place, but rather, gravity is always pulling at it to spill everything. Because of this, the soil in the bed puts pressure on the frame. The taller the bed is, the more pressure there is. A weaker wood might work fine for a foot tall garden bed, but the pressure of a three-foot-tall bed may shatter the wood and spill all over your yard. The taller the bed is, the thicker the wood that needs to be used. Other materials like concrete can also be used, but these will present their problems.

So, the secret to a perfectly sized raised garden bed is to keep it at least a foot tall and no more than four feet wide. Beyond that, you are free to do as you want. Just remember that more soil equals more pressure on the frame. Speaking of frames…

Why It Is Suitable for You

Companion planting works perfectly in raised beds. Those vegetables which need more space for their roots like carrots should be planted on top while others like leeks and onions will fill up space on the sides of your beds. The leeks and onions repel pests and will act as a shield for the carrot plants on the top of the bed.

CHAPTER 9:

Tips for Successful Raised Bed Gardening

Planting

The thrilling aspect of starting up an organic garden is the picking of plants. There are options for picking organic seeds or saplings that are dependent on the season. If you want a purely organic garden, don't pick the conventional plants that are raised with non-organic compost. If you purchase from the nursery, there is a definite way of determining if the sapling has been grown properly. The root bulb should have the same depth as your organic patch's hole. Its width should be twice as that. At the first plant, water it thoroughly then includes your organic compost that's about 3 inches deep.

Organic garden beds should be created with care to reduce any risk of plant diseases and pests that are soil-borne. Grow similar plants in the same garden beds and rotate the beds every year. For example, in your bed, one can have peas and beans. Bed two will be eggplants and tomatoes. Bed three is for turnips and carrots. The fourth bed contains squashes and cucumbers. Have a rotation system for each bed each year.

Spacing is essential to increase the plants' susceptibility to disease, intensify light reception, and increase the air circulation. Plants like tomatoes need a stake to keep them from touching the ground. This will expose the plant to extra sunshine and reduce the risk of any disease from the soil.

If you want fruit-bearing trees for your garden, pick the variety that is suitable for the environment and weather. Lemons and oranges are the types of fruit trees that can be grown in almost any type of location. Cherries and apples, on the other hand, will do well in colder conditions. The tropical climate is the best match for avocado and mango. Bear in mind the size of your garden or yard as most of these trees will have their roots clinging deep and long.

Spacing Between Plants

You can adhere to the typical garden plant spacing, which is in rows, or you might choose the square foot gardening that helps you use most of your space. This is done through marking off the garden bed in 12-inch square sections. Then you can start planting your seeds, one type of plant for each square. You can make a personalized diagram of your beds, so you know which plants you have planted in every square.

Position Plants Strategically

It is recommended that you put plants that need less care in the middle part of the bed and those that require more care on the edges. If only one side of your raised bed garden can be reached by sunlight, you need to do two things. Place the smaller ones toward the southern part and the taller plants on the northern part. If you are planting cucumbers, position them near the edge of the bed to allow them to trail over the side.

Determine the Right Depth

It is necessary to determine the right depth for the crop that you are trying to grow. To begin, you have to know that a minimum of 6 inches deep is necessary for most vegetables to grow well above ground. For root vegetables, a depth of 10 to 12 inches is necessary. However, some crops don't need to be covered with thick soil. If you are planting lettuce, you need to make a one-half inch deep furrow before sprinkling the seeds into every hole. You may then sprinkle a thin layer of soil to cover the lettuce seeds. If you are planting carrots, cover the seeds with fine-textured potting soil.

Practice Companion Planting

Just like other gardening methods, you can also take advantage of companion planting to reduce the risk of pest infestation. Allow compatible plants to grow close together and benefit from one another. You can plant beans with corn to increase nitrogen supply or with borage to repel worms in tomatoes. You can also grow peppers with spinach in between. This will allow the peppers to provide shade to the spinach and extend its picking season to make it

.more delicious.

Water and Mulch Your Garden after Planting

After planting your crop, nourish it with adequate amounts of water. Makes sure that the soil is only moistened, not drenched. You also need to mulch your garden with wood chips, leaves, straw, or grass clippings to keep the soil moist and prevent weeds.

Weed Management

Weeds are unwanted plants in the garden. If not properly managed, they can damage crops a lot worse than other garden pests. Controlling them is one of the biggest challenges in organic farming. The first step to weed control is becoming aware of the types of weeds that will grow on your farm. That way, you'd know how to deal with them effectively. A long-term plan should be taken into consideration when controlling weeds. It is easy to get rid of them in conventional farming, but the use of chemicals is not allowed in organic farms.

Take Good Care of Your Soil

If you've taken good care of your soil, your plants will turn out to be great. If not, you'll be growing low-quality plants. Some people tend to have a soil of high quality, but because they do not take good care of it, they end up ruining everything, and their soils get infected. Before they know it, this ends up affecting their plants, crops, and flowers too.

The importance of taking care of your soil cannot be stressed enough. Make use of additives if you must. Plants grown in raised beds tend to have 'limited options' when it comes to nutrients because these are secluded from the surrounding soil. So, they only have access to the nutrients available in the soil that you've planted these in. Stock up on nutrients so that you can add these to the soil whenever you see signs that you need to do so.

Check the Soil for Drainage

If water seeps too fast through it, that means your soil won't benefit from rainfall, and if the water stands for too long, that, too, will be harmful to your soil. Water that stands for too long may infect your plants, especially if it is contaminated water. Another thing you can do is take some soil in your hands and squeeze it so that it forms a ball. If your soil does not form a ball, that means that your soil's too sandy. If it breaks into several little pieces (or if it crumbles), that means your soil can be used to grow plants and that it can retain healthy amounts of water. This also means that your soil is perfect for plant growth.

Companion Gardening

Adding plants that complement each other has many benefits, such as helping to protect your plants from pests and insects like mosquitoes, grasshoppers, **etc.** Growing plants that counteract these conditions will allow you to avoid using dangerous insecticides. Bloodflower is a great herb for those of you who need to get rid of worms. While worms are great for the soil, if you feel that there are way too many worms in your soil, this herb is just what you need to protect your soil. Tansy would help get rid of mosquitoes and grasshoppers too. There are several other herbs you could grow.

Importance of Nitrogen

Nitrogen is so essential for plants because it is what plants use when they are photosynthesizing. Always use cash crops to enrich the oxygen content in your soil. You don't want to wait till your plants get yellow and show signs of nitrogen deficiency, because that means it is too late. You want to take good care of your plants and your soil. Do your plants and yourself a favor by planting cash crops after you have grown vegetables, flowers, and plants in the soil. Go for crop rotation if you must.

Avoid Overwatering

In the summertime, go easy on the water. This is when your plants grow. Don't overwater the soil around this period. You should only do so once or twice a day. Any more than that might prove to be harmful and possibly drown your plants—something you want to avoid.

Growing Plants Together

You want to protect the soil; if you grow the plants together, they will be able to shelter the soil underneath them. This will protect the soil from evaporation, and this will also help get rid of weeds. You won't need to mulch all over again, either.

Subdivide Your Garden

Plan on how you intend to use the soil. You could grow peppers, carrots, and peas on one side while growing onions and cucumbers on the other. You could also choose to grow vegetables on one side and flowers and fruits on the other.

Always Be Prepared

Know that this is what you want, or else you are just wasting your time. While raised-bed gardening may seem like an appealing idea, it also involves a lot of work, so you just want to go for it and be consistent. You'd be wasting a lot of money and time otherwise.

Choose Quality Building Products

Be careful of what you are buying when it comes to purchasing wood for the bed or when it comes to purchasing topsoil for your raised-bed garden. Any material with preservatives could cause more damage than insects, pests, and insecticides combined because these preservatives tend to seep into the water and can ruin your plants completely.

Soil Maintenance

Upgrading your soil

Having the right soil conditions is fundamental if you need your plants to perform at their best. A few plants have distinct necessities as far as the level of causticity or alkalinity that they will flourish in; however, most garden plants like unbiased conditions and will endure somewhat acidic or soluble varieties. It is worth checking the pH level of your soil first to see if it is exceedingly acidic or neutral.

Know your soil

Basic soil testing packs can be purchased on the web or from most garden stores. They are straightforward to utilize and will ask you to recognize which plants your soil or manure will suit. An example of soil or manure is stirred up in a testing arrangement, and the shading the fluid changes to is at that point checked on the shading outline. 1 is amazingly acidic, and 14 are neutral; A pH of 7 is unbiased. It is prudent to take a couple of tests from various areas of the raised bed to ensure an accurate reading is being taken.

Corrosive soil

Adding compost to the soil can bring down the pH with the goal that it is increasingly acidic. If your soil is on the neutral side and you need to grow corrosive adoring plants, this progression is vital, and, in most gardens, this is enough. Make your acidic compost at home by including heaps of spoiled pine needles, woodchips, sawdust, decaying leaves, or even new espresso beans to the compost heap. It will, in the end, turn impartial once more, so it is worth verifying each year and garnish with increasingly acidic materials if necessary.

Alkaline soil

Including mushroom compost or hardwood debris to the manure can be a viable strategy for making progressively antacid conditions.

Then again, some items can be purchased, for example, ground limestone, ordinarily called "garden lime," which has the dynamic element of calcium carbonate.

Soil pH

Soil pH shows the sharpness or alkalinity of your soil on a scale of 1 to 14, with 7.0 being neutral. Soil with a pH lower than 7.0 is acidic, higher than 7.0 is alkaline.

Most consumable plants incline toward soil that is impartial to marginally acidic.

In exceptionally acidic or basic soil, plants have difficulty getting to supplements.

You can test the pH of your soil utilizing a pack acquired from a garden community or by sending a soil example to a lab.

Soil texture

Texture alludes to the mineral substance of the soil—precisely, the size of the mineral particles in the soil, and their relative extent to each other.

Particles are classified by size, from littlest to biggest, as mud, residue, and sand. The bigger the molecule size, the bigger the air pockets (known as pores) between them.

Pores permit water and air to travel through the soil, which is the reason sandy soil channel rapidly and mud soils will, in general, become hard and waterlogged. Residue falls somewhere between the two.

Compost

Utilizing compost is the absolute best thing you can accomplish for your garden—also that fertilizing the soil keeps an immense measure of drainage out of landfills. Use manure as mulch (spread it on the soil to hold weeds down, lessen dissipation and disintegration, and develop soil supplements), gardening soil to make an incredible holder blend, or add a bunch to planting openings before transplanting bushes or starts. Regardless of whether your open-air space is small or high over the ground, it's possible to make good manure. All you need is a little piece of the yard, a container structured particularly for composting, a grower on your deck, or even only a crate under your sink. Useful manure requires air, dampness, and a decent equalization of organic drainage materials.

Mulch

Close to including manure, mulching is the best thing you can improve for your soil. Mulch is a layer of material spread over the outside of your soil. Conventional mulches incorporate straw, compost, leaf form (leaf manure), and bark mulch; however, plastic sheeting, cardboard and paper, rocks, and even texture can likewise be utilized.

Mulching keeps weeds under control, shields the soil from disintegration, decreases decrease of nutrients, and goes about as a separator to ensure plants' foundations in winter and to direct the effects of blistering summer temperatures. Utilizing alluring mulches can give your holders or beds a newly planted look.

If you use compost as mulch, it will carry out twofold responsibility—giving all the defensive benefits, however adding nutrients to the soil also.

Plan to mulch your containers or garden beds, at any rate, two times per year: in spring, to give benefits during the dynamic constructing season and in tumble to ensure the soil over the winter. Spread a layer somewhere in the range of two and four, thick over the uncovered surfaces of your soil. The mulch ought not to touch the stem or trunk of a plant; leave a bit of breathing room. Mulch that sits against stems and stalks traps dampness and can support ailment and decay.

Fertilizing Your Raised Bed Garden

When you start seedlings indoors, you begin to fertilize them. When seedlings start to sprout outdoors, you fertilize them. As your plants grow and mature, you fertilize them. It is only just before you harvest any edible vegetables that you stop fertilizing them because you don't want to add any more liquid to the soil. Fertilizing your plants is an absolute must if you want beautiful flowers or large yields.

Fertilizer comes in two types. There are fertilizers such as manure, which can be added to and then mixed throughout the soil. A fertilizer like this is a useful application at the start of spring or end of fall. However, we can also mix in compost as a top layer with a blanket of mulch to protect our beds over the winter and add nutrients back into the soil. So we're not going to worry about fertilizers that mix into the soil. Instead, we're going to stick with liquid fertilizer.

There are many options when it comes to liquid fertilizers. Some gardeners brew what is called manure tea, which sounds as tasty as it smells. Another form of fertilizer is created by crushing comfrey until it oozes sap, which you distill in water and then feed your plants. For our purposes, we will be sticking to the store-bought liquid fertilizers, but even here, we have two options. The first option is to buy a premixed fertilizer. These are ones with the NPK ratio listed on them in numeric form like 30-30-30.

Knowing what these numbers mean makes it easy to understand these fertilizers. For most plants, select a fertilizer that is balanced around 30-30-30. This will provide a spread of nutrients to the plants—however, some vegetables like a lot of one particular nutrient. For example, onions like having lots of nitrogen, and so you may go with a nitrogen-heavy mixture with a ratio around 50-20-20. If you research your plants before seeding your gardens, then you can group those with specific macronutrient needs and feed them a separate fertilizer. If you are going with a general fertilizer, then you should stick with the 30-30-30, purchase whichever brand is the most attractive, and follow the instructions on the label for how much to dilute in water.

Spray or water your plants once every week or two, depending on the instructions of that particular brand. Always reduce the strength that you feed seedlings. Fertilizer should be applied directly to the soil around the plant and not all over the foliage itself. If the leaves of the plant start to curl back and show signs of nutrient damage, then you will want to flush the soil and dilute your fertilizer more. For the most part, applying fertilizer becomes as easy as watering your plants, but you should be mindful of taking a pH reading of the soil from time to time. Your local gardening center will have plenty of soil pH test kits that you can purchase and use to make sure that the levels in your soil aren't off the charts. Too much and too little will make it impossible for your plants to use the nutrients in the soil properly and this can cause some significant damage to your plants. It's always better to start a fertilizer routine at a weaker dosage and work up to the perfect level rather than overshoot it and hurt the plants.

Watering Your Raised Bed Garden

Water is life. This is the truth among all living things, including plants. Your garden will need equal nourishment from the sun and water. You can make the most out of your water supply by water targeting, utilizing water butts, and mulching of the beds.

It is best to water the plants in the morning or the evening. That way, plants will absorb all the moisture before the hottest time of the day hits. Target your watering areas and determine what part of the plants needs most water. This means watering the soil that is just above the roots. Do not soak the plant because some moisture will not be absorbed but will just evaporate.

If you built your raised bed garden properly then watering, it is going to be just as easy as watering any plants you grow outside. You are going to find that you need to water them a little bit more often than those in the ground but only by the slimmest of margins. Plants grown in containers tend to need to be watered more often, and raised bed gardens are no different. But they're much more significant and this slows down the process to the point where it won't be very noticeable. However, if you haven't appropriately built drainage holes into your raised garden bed frame, then watering is going to make for a much more complicated experience. While raised beds do offer plants better protection from issues like root rot, a poor design can wipe that protection out and leave you with rotting plants.

Building drainage holes into your raised bed frame isn't very complicated. You can use a drill to add holes or cut out a slit along the width. Whatever method you choose to use, this will open up your raised bed garden to the outside environment. We use some netting over the hole so that the water can drain, but lifeforms have a much harder time getting in. This doesn't prevent critters entirely, but it does reduce the frequency. One of the best features of raised bed gardens is improved drainage. But if you create an environment in which water gets trapped in the soil, then you are putting your plants in danger. It is always better to err on the side of dry rather than wet, and you need to be mindful of this starting from the design of your raised bed frame itself.

Another way we avoid having water stay in our soil too long is to water our plants in the morning. One of the biggest helpers we have when it comes to keeping our plants dry is the sun. While we need water to properly drain out from the bottom of our raised garden beds, we also need the sun to evaporate water, so it leaves from the top. This act of evaporation only happens when the sun is out, and so watering plants at night is a terrible idea. When you do water at night, the water never leaves the soil from the top, and so it can get stuck in the bed. Doing this once might not kill your plants, but if you make it a habit, it surely will. You should water the first thing in the morning. If this isn't possible, then try to water your raised beds before noon.

The question of how often you should water your plants is going to depend on what those plants are. Some only need to be watered once a week, and others need to be watered twice, maybe even three times a week. There are a couple of factors that will help to determine if you need to water more often or less often, but there is a general rule of thumb that gives you an accurate measurement of if you should water them or not. The finger test is one of the oldest gardening techniques we have, and yet it continues to be one of the most useful even after centuries. Simply take a finger and stick it an inch into the soil. If it feels moist, then it isn't time to water. If it doesn't feel moist, then pull your finger out and take a look at it. If there is any soil clinging to it, then it is still a little moist, and you should wait. If there isn't, then it is time to water the plants. This technique will sometimes be performed at half an inch rather than an inch, depending on the plant being grown.

Using the finger test will tell you if it is time to water them or not. You may quickly get into a rhythm of how often you need to water your raised beds, but you need to be careful not to get too confident if it is your first-time gardening. The temperature is going to change throughout the growing period, and this is going to affect the rate of watering. Keep applying the finger test every day during your crop so that you understand what a garden bed goes through with the seasons and as the plants mature and come to harvest. The higher the temperature, the quicker the soil is going to dry out, and the more you will have to water your plants.

Conclusion

Gardening is good therapy. There are several therapeutic aspects of gardening. The quietness of working among the flowers and/or vegetables is proven to slow our breathing and help us relax both mentally and physically. Quiet time in the garden also allows us to restructure our thoughts and work things out in our minds. It's hard to stay mad or feel like there's nothing right in your world when you are surrounded by the sight and smell of flowers and/or knowing that before long, you'll be eating the things you've helped grow.

Another possible therapeutic aspect of gardening is that it can help you release some pent-up frustration and stress. For example, a friend of mine takes a great deal of pleasure in cutting the corn stalks in one of her extensive gardens after the corn has been harvested. She covets this job each year. It's one of those things that makes momma happy.

You may well be wondering why on earth, a raised bed garden is any easier than planting vegetables straight into the soil. Or why indeed I have titled this as I have done, by mentioning that raised bed gardening is easy.

Well, the fact is that in my opinion, growing vegetables in a raised bed is by far the easiest way of growing great vegetables without the considerable labor involved when growing the traditional way.

Now, most of the work is done, and the fun part starts. While you wait for your veggies to grow, a little attention is needed; water them regularly and keep your eyes peeled for any pests or weeds. Then wait for the fruit to mature and start harvesting!

Growing vegetables in raised beds make gardening a pleasure. With limited time and space, you can grow an abundance of food in a small area. The benefits are numerous; fewer weeds and pests, better drainage, better soil, no compacting of the soil, less pain potential for you, the gardener, to name but a few. Your friends will envy your neat, attractive garden and harvest of healthy, tasty vegetables.

Now that you have all the information needed, it is time to get going. Walk around your available space during the day to find a sunny location. Once you have decided where you want to place your raised bed, decide on the size and dimensions. The next step is to make a list of everything you will need, from the soil, compost, and other materials, to the frames. Once your bed is up and filled up with the soil mixture, it is time to turn your attention to the plants. Select the type of veggies you want to grow according to the guidelines I have provided. If you want to grow plants from seeds, you will have to do some prior planning since it will take time for them to develop into seedlings ready to be planted outside in your box. Otherwise, you can purchase seedlings to plant directly into your raised beds.

Raised beds are high if you are growing in an area with poor soil. One part of my vegetable plot was about three inches of soil on top of hard-core rubble, which isn't ideal for planting anything in. If your soil is poor, lacking in nutrients, or has any problems, then a raised bed is ideal because instead of amending all the soil in your vegetable garden, you can amend the soil within the raised bed and leave the rest alone. Amending the soil for the whole plot can be very time consuming and quite expensive, yet with a raised bed, you can just amend a small area at a time, making it more manageable.

Other benefits of raised bed gardening include:

Better for your back – if you struggle to bend then a raised bed can be built as high as you need so that you do not need to spend a lot of time bending

Ideal for wheelchair gardeners – if you are in a wheelchair and want to garden, then raised beds are ideal because you can build them so they can be reached from your wheelchair. When built the right height and width, the entire vegetable garden can be managed from your wheelchair

Made in the USA
Middletown, DE
04 December 2020